language
MINE

language
MINE

SABRINA PAMELA WRIGHT

iUniverse, Inc.
New York   Bloomington

Language Mine

Copyright © 2010 by Sabrina Pamela Wright

iUniverse books may be ordered through booksellers or by contacting:
iUniverse
1663 Liberty Drive
Bloomington, IN 47403
www.iuniverse.com
1-800-Authors (1-800-288-4677)

Because of the dynamic nature of the Internet, any Web addresses or links contained in this book may have changed since publication and may no longer be valid. The views expressed in this work are solely those of the author and do not necessarily reflect the views of the publisher, and the publisher hereby disclaims any responsibility for them.

ISBN: 978-1-4502-2117-7 (pbk)
ISBN: 978-1-4502-2118-4 (ebk)

Printed in the United States of America
iUniverse rev. date: 10/06/2010

Dedication

To my family, Sybil, Barbara, Antoinette and little Olivia,

You do not hesitate to share your strength with me and champion my endeavours. Your existence keeps me afloat, everyday.

To the villains and heroes, perfect and marred in all tenses of time, your inspiration is unparalleled.

Contents

Introduction

Walking alone on a busy street, you are marked by an onlooker and "your name" is called. All there is in a name, through experience and relationship, from what you believe it to be, to what the caller calls it to be is cast, on you and only accepted through acknowledgement. Pay no attention, and the shadowy spotlight is shed, you can continue live in the gaps.

"Deconstruction is not a dismantling of the structure of a text, but a demonstration that it has already dismantled itself. Its apparently-solid ground is no rock, but thin air."

– J. Hillis Miller

Working on this collection over several years has seen its purpose morph, various meanings emerge, and different structures sculpted. After the final edit a collection about the construction and destruction of the idea of self remains. The ideas it challenges are the ideologies we hold in our web of beliefs, the ones that keep us connected to our society and to our sanity. It discusses personal understandings of human interactions and emotions. All of the musings create a piece that illustrates the clarity that comes from deconstructing views of self, experiences of love, anguish and creativity, the responsibilities of being a member of society and of being the "other".

As a teacher who took that job seriously said, "Mine language. Language the mine." – Dunja Baus

This is my first excavation.

...scrapped and remodeled, again...again...

Naked

Gender scripts
Sell out
Under
suggestive
Billboard lights,
Suit up
Under
mirrored
Fluorescent lights,
Play out
Under
scrutinizing
Spotlights.
Staged is the
construct of you
and reducible to
a dictionary definition.
Strip me of
my costume
and behold
that identity is blank
not born.

Language Mine

Don't

Need
between the lines
Weave
between landmine lines
Live
within ruled sheets
Linger
within twenty-three blue borders
Less legally permitted.

Move
only when the page is turned
When
ever it is turned
Whom
ever overturns it
How
ever they bend it
into
stylistic subservience.

In the margins we

Mine Language

Cross

                    double red lines into
                  a subversive country—

Thrive

                on ink notes on our hands
          and on torn paper napkins—

Grasp

          through midnight shadows
            for mangled notepads—

Progress

           only on slants and contours.
        Unafraid of the blank page
                     which

Shows

       starkly that although trained
           we're neither straight
               nor narrow,

Speak

             only in free-hand
        to create a free-verse

Manifesto.

Half-breed

Inseminated by biology,
Shifted in geography,
Breed a biography
and
Muddle up history.
Soldiers of otherness,
fight to fit and fall
in the infamous Battle of Displacement.
Victoriously
force names on the nameless and
exile for the misfits.

Lyricism

because of lethargy,
anger, heart   beats
in   justice
of the night
you-me, possession, him-her, barriers of
language, anguish, tears, salty
crackers, oreos, race, -isms, politics
caricatures that characterize characters.
Crying v. laughing
Living v. breathing
Sleeping v. dreaming
in the sunlight
my son, your daughter, our family, one life,
multiplicity, metamorphosis, mortality:
movement.

Amnesia

Amnesia
you are a dream.
Cannot remember
Yesterday
seemed
The end of the world was on the verge
but, today everything's alive.
Cannot see through
Tomorrow
seems
The end of the world is on its way
but, everything's alive today.
Can't remember
why the ill-temper,
why the concern,
why the emotion,
But shit! I'm alive today!
You are mine
Amnesia.

There is No Truth

Only
Fragments and Selections,
Self-Deception and Perception,
Memory and Meaning,
Sugar Coatings and Motivations,
Moods and Colouring,
Dreams and Neuroses,
Love and Hate,
Innuendo and Ideology,
Psychoanalysis.
Relativity and Promises,
Action and Blindness,
Whispers and Words,
Everything in between,
Backtracking on all of it,
Returning for another round and
What's left is Mathematics.

Know-it-all

In the beginning
I know I know and
Confidence bears a foundation.
Halfway through
I knew I knew but
Doubt shakes the organization.
At the end of it all
I'm sure I'm not sure
I'm forced to rethink the situation.

Decided in the Middle

Decided to change
middle of the day,
not at the sound of alarm.
Decided to change
middle of the year,
though resolutions are not yet due.

Decided to live
middle of the night,
eyelids flicker with dreams.
Decided to live
middle of the month,
the leaves haven't begun to turn.

Decided to grow
middle of the street,
the traffic lights blind a bright red.
Decided to grow
middle of a book,
the story will never finish.

Decided to be
middle of a minute,
the time is half-past now,

Decided to think
middle of this change,
and instantly I trigger

...scars are experiences on your skin...

Divine

Imperfection you are my saviour.
Karma you are my queen.
It's the balance that you keep,
the bounced cheque that you write
that makes it all divine.

Weakness you are my shelter.
Fate you are my way home.
It's the choice that you give,
the no-refund policy you write
that makes it all divine.

I die everyday of a broken spirit.
Crushed each time
by the weight of my ego.
Reincarnated everyday as a human –
And that makes it all divine.

Humiliation you are my friend.
Humility you are my soul.
And the reason it's divine,
What keeps it all divine –

Is that it's not...

Phantom Woman

Invade mental cavity
Haunt my space
Confuse me with the question
Of your presence.
Whisper echoes
in my ear
stealthily stalk
then disappear.
Phantom Woman
I suspect you are only that?

History

Countless
Years
That
Bind
And
The moment that
Breaks
Love
Is the emotion
That turns
Into
Hate.

Cloned

Resemblance
Intangible.
No match
In the pigment
Of our eyes.

We

Converge
Through the moon in Pisces,

Diverge
When telling *his*tory,

Emerge
With stark differences

that threaten existence and
deafen this persuasive tongue.

No father and know me.
Know mother and no you.

So where is the imposter?
Who is the clone?

You –
Or dare I say
Me.

The F Word

No static meaning –
a fill-in, stand in
for the real
and overused
to satisfy the emptiness
that has no name.
A visitor
that held you last night?
Or the best of
who disappoints last time?
Revoke the license to arbitrate,
assign obligation,
assassinate.
As powerful as the L word
so it is abused deliberately
just as these lines are misused
to present
sweetly wrapped vulgarity.
Fuck, it's too much to say
But it slides from these lips anyway...
smirk at each another and turn away
Friend.

Spring Cleaning

Need a new closet,
Cause you're wearin' all my clothes,
Tossin' round my dirty laundry,
Crushin' all my boney toes.

Shackled

Can't you
See these silver links
Rusty and rubbing
Depreciating
Against the flesh
Of our desires?
Raise a hand to
Shield your abuse.
Catch your lies.
Punch your face.
Retaliate.
But these chains they clench,
Deprecate
they burn and bond
when we reach –
spreads the belief
that we can't get free
'cause we're
mentally medicated
slaves of creed.

Lifeline

Lifeline,
navigate the
scars in hand
where they re
move numbness
etched by servitude.

Depth,
dive into
lips that stammer
for words that
shear chipped teeth
unearthed by fists.

Pulse,
vibrate in
ears that bleed
to stitch hearing
previously
sliced with slurs.

infinity answers
the equations
you create to evaluate
and the assumption
in your smarmy smile
writes me a cheque.

summed up in your case number
puzzle complete.

Collisions

I took your
Life in my hands
Crushed it
With every
Muscle in my grip

When I
Crashed
That car
When I
Smashed
My liver
When we
Clashed
At dinner

And we
Broke
All those dishes

Bloody bruises
Beaten
Into your skin
Banged
Into my mind
Busted up
Your spine

Wish we could switch
My mere lip stitched
You never forgave
I never forget

...the games we play...

City Burb

This city corrupts.
Nothing like
my Burb
all the houses
all in a row and
all the schools
are named after
Churches,
which are named after
Saints,
who are essentially just
People.
Where the mayor
will soon be canonized
and strip clubs are disowned
or zoned
on the outskirts
of town.
Lifestyle
validated only by
the existence
of fairytales.
Only the trees have grown
the prices multiplied,
ignorance amplified
and the lone town bum
was forced into hiding years ago.
So we're
Buying in the burbs,
We're hiding in the burbs,
We're dying in the burbs,
just pretend.

Cardiac Arrest

Soundly aloof,
yet dangerously restless.
Irregular heartbeats
provide a pulse for paranoia
and phobic ponderings
push through.
The site of dislocation
is this tightness in chest
that comes from small talk.
Signals of unnerving awareness
shoot down the arm of sociality,
extend through a handshake,
and gives a jolt of electric energy
that kills.

The Diet

Starved by superficialities,
eating only when you weren't around
to take me out for gossip and beer.
Provisions must be made
as a sterile season approaches,
so I'm rummaging through remnants to find
the last stimulating meal.
Meticulously phase out shallow calories
and eat in obscure restaurants
with someone who will exchange omegas
and organic ideas.
No more counting the calories you serve and
ending up with a negative number.
No more deciding if you're stingy or just deficient.
Need a taste
that will fire up my tongue
and feed my brain
instead of
straining it through a sieve.

Corporate Rhymes

Lesson One
Share: Offer your seat when commuting

Lesson Seven
Master your timetable: Juggle time and money

Lesson Ten:
Credit Management: Sign away your soul

Lesson Fourteen
See the Guidance Counselor: Get used to rejection by
appearance and success by resume

Lesson Twenty-One
Choose a Specialization: Defeat and competition

Lesson Twenty-Eight
Develop your thesis: How to manipulate words without saying
a word

But your diploma reads:
"rhymes and fables made it all okay,
don't forget the games we played
blindfold, disorient, send 'em to kill
thrash 'em 'til the riches spill"

Take that nigger, that fag, that cunt joke to the boardroom.
Cash that gossip in for a promotion.
Pad that paycheque with catch phrases.
Delegate blame through a game of "it".

You're tagged
and now I can be president.

Circus

Imitation
you do not flatter me
when I am likened
to a monkey.

Sleuth of costume parties
erupt
under a mountain of education
where they are
mocking shadows of us
that we cast in music videos.
These performers
good only as
understudies for
the maple syrup lady.

Free admission
to all who can
Suck smoke from a splif
Or juggle baby fathers
And blackball
none.

No Longer in Service

Connect by sound wave.
Meet through pixels.
Bond by profile.
Con verse by text.
Console by e-mail.
A thousand clicks and we're all friends.

See you on a crowded train,
Falling asleep on my shoulder,
Hold me up when the train stops,
Turn my nose up if you smell,
Turn your nose down if the language
I speak is unknown to you.

Touch my bumper in traffic,
Lock eyes in the rear view,
Curse you like we sleep together
But, there's no recognition
Just glazed eyes
That can't match real to digital.

So two million souls are in the streets
Just passing through when we meet.

Blood in Our Hands

So why can't your god write this scope of horror?
Or my god speak through tongues and tea leaves?
And our God be not at all?

Compelled to conceal by the book that reveals,
Quietly suffering like Job at our jobs,
Testaments justify why we kill those who won't testify.

It's our hands.
The blood in our hands,
The blood on our hands
Destructs
Constructs
faith and blasphemy.

By Jane Doe

You've traveled the world,
the letters after shadow your name.

It says you fucked your teacher,
It says you swore on profanities.

And when you die
The tombstone will read,
"Loved always"
But it won't say
"Except by..."

Reduced to a
Highlight reel,

Lowlights
Bring out your green eyes.

Make sure you always wear clean panties.
Make sure you have a crafted edit-or
rely on

Resumes and bios,
Sound   bites and essays,

That's it.
Good-bye Jane Doe.

The Secret Society of Sobriety

Watching me sober up
seeing that I
disappear before your eyes,
so now we're strangers...

...yet I feel–stranger–
pouring logic
into a state of hyper-reality
connects us through our disconnection,
makes the fun house fun,
makes you clowns seem witty
and all avenues
are paved with brick, stained urine
Alice and all her friends were there
and you were there
and you were there
so now we're familiar...

...yet I am a stranger.

Raising the Bar

It gets higher
each time
you fall
below—
a reverse
game of
limbo.

Debt or Alive

Penny, quarter, nickel, dime
why do I spend so much time
wasted.

Dreaming up the taste
of a slice of pie
promised—
work that dollar
honest -or not-
paying you in happy,
drains quickly sole currency

I sweat that dollar today
and thought that Friday
must be easier with equal pay

Now

A twenty, a fifty, a hundred, a thousand lay in hand,
the other is caught in whip cream quick sand—
that cherry red Ferrari on top 'aint free miss.
Just add it to my laundry list
'cuz it seems Forever carries this stressful load
of always giving in
get-by mode.

Alienation

Made a wrong turn.
Landed on this planet.
Subject to foreign policies.
Dragged to a room.
Experimental probes question
X-rays expose nothing.
Locked in a cage
Inquiries of how I work
Had small almond eyes
Over five feet tall
And dressed in
strange white coats
polyester
skin peach pigment
Unlike the shades of grey
I'm used to
Memories fade
Trauma ensues
Maybe hypnosis
Will jog my memory

Shadowboxing

Thrust forward as a
low blow to the lower back
deals an intense sting.

Quick. Regroup.

Cuz' here comes
upper cut
left hook
right jab
jab-jab-jab
who arrive with vertigo.

Strategic lyric shuffle
makes you stumble back so
shaded nemesis grows tall,
warps the perspective—threat.

Cloaked adversary twists out a
technical knock out.

Ding, Ding, Ding, bell rings
house lights go up to reveal
not a trounced or tangible opponent—
just you, playin' yourself.

....like clarity + electricity...

The Lottery

Struck by a bolt—
astronomical odds.
6 billion and counting to one.
A favour of Fate tightly intertwines,
chemically connects
the counted two, one soully
As others part,
broken by the
wind that flies coldly between.
They speak on the same wavelength
move to each other's vibration.
Lovers are unshakable,
So tightly intertwined,
So chemically connected,
the wind can't pass through them.

Sour Times

It went sour.
He stayed past due.
Drunk her beauty.
Thirst made it sweet
for a split 'til
spread the smell,
her selfish stink.
Admitted,
that hard lump
on which he forced a swallow,
was her distasteful heart.
The attractive package masked
a transformation from silk to curds.
Before the date due
he was cheated, defrauded
and tasted something
that made his stomach churn.
His mouth pondered the last sickening sip
decided disgust and
spat what he almost tried to spare.

The Conductor's Opus

Baton of wood
cuts like a knife
into mental space
to make jumbled notes
of her physical pace
so he can play his fiddle
and dance after it.

Misunderstanding

Understanding
Is
Not
Wishy washy
Pish Posh
Mish Mash
Tit for Tat
Toe to Toe
E-ni, Me-ni or
My-ni Mo
As the saying goes
Right or Wrong
Yours or Mine
Me or you
In Timbuktu
Or God knows where
Blank stare.

Ruined

revive my soul You
the wind that moves me
yet stealing breath.
create my laugh You
the smile in my solitude.
want you every second I
need you every moment in between.
shudder at the thought of your absence I
shudder at the spirit of your fingertips and
the presence of your touch.
Heartbeat quickens.
It's all I can do to not think of you.
Ignorance deserted me the day I met you
and now forever—
I am in ruin.

Move me

I challenge you
Not to talk to
Gaze at
Or impress.
Not to enchant,
Lure
Or bamboozle.
Not to judge,
Order and
Expect.
Not to love,
Want,
Or want me to want you.
Don't change
Shift,
Or relocate me.

Stir.
Move me.

I dare you.

Don't Question Love

In the elusive world outside the stratosphere
It constructs the cosmos alongside chance.
Not in our minds, our hearts or our hands
lies it unqualified, not quantified, complete.
Far beyond linguistic limits—
an intense wordlessness
when named
will either glow or combust.
See it behind the pane of my eyes.
See it behind the pane of yours.
And when it shines through and deflects,
it reflects
shades spliced and split with shards.
And so makes a question of truth
not Love's
but ours.

Love Letter of David

the Hunter shoots,
ruptures this heart,
penetrates this flesh,
searing
passion and pain.

all I can do is
leak from the eyes
fall to my knees
bleed from the chest

smear it on your sleeve
and cheeks,
the rite of a tribe.

beg for more
oh Mercy!
like a good little masochist

paraded for all to believe the
rapturous wound of your love.

Love Letter of Goliath

Fight for numbness.
Crusade for fear.
Teach past tense.
Preach denial,
high on a stool
in a corner
of the mind
where you
sit
sent
punished.

incorruptible lies
about love
not lost between us
we quit
yet spit,
"it was
intended
expected
accepted"

but dejected?

not affected!

No admission that
together we are essential
individuals

still splintered.

Scar Tissue

Original tissue is only 20% stronger so
With a fresh needle, not so clean, I struggle to re-stitch,
The flesh did not bust when I took us in, lonesome and
nomadic,
Only as we choose to nourish and play out those words
spoken in uncertain times.
Now there's a re-opening for the more tortures of no
guarantee
(which you should not say will not be)
Heal! this ailment Learn!
Or ever will it bruise and scar, fester and churn, scar and
bruise, blister and burn
Good thing there is no more blood
Phase number seventy seven of wound healing through
And almost–
On to the next one.

6th Scent

Can't be sold
But should be bottled
the
Chemically enhancing
smell of the dew
that is
your skin.

Wet.

Leave a piece
In the fibres of
My life.
My bed.
My sheets.
My head.

Alive

in your scent
that
smells like tranquility
smells like I'm home
smells like
      every
           good
                memory
Like clarity + electricity
Like my sixth sense is kicking in
muting all others.